7

Steps

To an

Integrated

&

Implementable

Marketing

Plan

Shark Bite Coaching

ISBN: 061584815X
ISBN-13: 978-0615848150

DEDICATION

This book is dedicated to entrepreneurs and business professionals who are ready to take their businesses to the next level.

I wish you luck in your success and hope that I can help even just a little bit.

CONTENTS

INTRODUCTION

Managing and growing your own business doesn't just stop at selling products and services, for how else will people find out about what you have to offer if you don't market it? Marketing is the task of introducing your company to your target customers. It is when you find ways to make your products and services stand out and creating your own distinctive niche in the market, allowing you to stand out.

Marketing your business will make you more easily recognizable. There are many companies selling similar products and services, but the way you use marketing techniques and strategies will have a huge impact on the success of your small business. You may think that carrying out your marketing strategies is the toughest part, but equally challenging is deciding what marketing strategies you will implement.

To get on the easiest road to marketing your products and services successfully, you need to have your own marketing plan. Your marketing plan is the result of your decisions regarding strategies and techniques and how best to execute them. In fact, countless successful entrepreneurs will agree with the saying: "If you want to be successful, create your own marketing plan."

If you are a start-up business owner, the last thing you may want to do is face another tough task, especially one that seems as difficult to complete as the development of a marketing plan. However, a marketing plan doesn't have to be hundreds of pages long; a small business won't need an inch-thick workbook to succeed. The more concise and current your marketing plan, the better.

This guide will teach you the seven key steps to ultimately generate an integrated and implementable marketing plan, one that will prove essential to the growth and overall success of your business. And once your marketing goals and visions start becoming reality, your journey on the road to inevitable success will be much more enjoyable.

WHY DO YOU NEED A MARKETING PLAN?

How does a marketing plan differ from a business plan?

A business plan covers everything about your business, such as your history, vision statement, contact information, product and service details, etc. It is actually the perfect guide for creating your marketing plan since it will help you determine which strategies will best suit your business goals.

A marketing plan, meanwhile, focuses only on your marketing goals, strategies, visions and steps. You don't just make a list of what you want to do when marketing your company—you will also need to detail how you will accomplish these tasks. However, the planning doesn't stop with the strategies; you also need to understand how to implement them correctly.

In short, your business plan will guide you in the creation of an integrated marketing plan personalized for your company, and in turn your marketing plan will guide you on the best path to success for your business.

It will also be helpful to understand the definitions of some key terminology such as marketing planning, marketing plan, and integrated marketing plan.

Marketing Planning: This is the process of researching and analyzing the market and the economic situation, and then developing objectives, strategies, and plans that are suited to your business' resources, competency, mission, and objectives. This will then be followed by implementation, evaluation, and adjustments (as needed) to achieve the established objectives.

Marketing Plan: This is the file that summarizes the knowledge, strategies, and specific plans to be used in achieving the objectives reached through the marketing planning process.

Integrated Marketing Plan: The result of an overall, comprehensive planning process which considers ALL aspects of the organization and how they can work together to create a more cohesive approach to completing the established objectives and successfully achieving your overall business goals.

WHAT YOU WILL NEED TO WRITE IT

No matter how you organize your marketing plan, it should be easily understood by all. You want to ensure that everyone in the company has access to the document physically and will understand the means and methods described.

There is vital information needed prior to writing a marketing plan. If you have everything you need before you sit down to write, you will avoid interrupting the writing and thinking processes, and, basically, save time. Here is what you should have when preparing to write your marketing plan:

Financial Reports: These should cover profit and loss, operating budget and recent sales figures relating to each product and region for the current year as well as the past three years. If your company is new, you should have financial reports for as long as your company has been in business, or at least an estimate of the reports.

Product/Service Inventory: You must have a complete and detailed inventory of your existing products and services including the target markets associated with each. If you are planning to launch a new product or service, it is even more imperative to have a complete list so it can be appropriately budgeted for.

Organization Chart: You should have an organization chart handy—especially for larger companies. If your company has fewer than five employees, you may not need this section right away, but if you plan to grow [that IS the point of all this, right?], then you should include a section as a placeholder for future use.

COMPONENTS OF A MARKETING PLAN

These are the components of a marketing plan:

- mission statement
- executive summary
- external and internal analysis
- current marketing situation
- objectives and issues
- target market
- marketing strategies
- marketing programs
- financial plans
- implementation controls

Mission Statement: The mission statement should contain a clear description of your business, what it stands for, and the marketing goals you want to accomplish. Your marketing mission statement should be based on your business plan mission statement but with a marketing slant to it. It should also be easy to comprehend.

Executive Summary: The executive summary acts as an overview of the key objectives of your plan. It should be brief and readable, comprising a single page located at the front of the marketing plan. Sentences should be short and bullet points used for important concerns.

The executive summary is intended to portray a concise description of the upcoming plans detailed in the document while reducing your main thoughts to brief statements. It is usually easier to write this section after the completion of the marketing plan.

External and Internal Analyses: External analysis includes the economy, the demographics, trends, competition, and target markets which affect your business from the outside. Internal analysis provides an inside look at your company such as the current financial state, your future marketing plans, and the strengths and weaknesses of the company. The business world will offer opportunities as well as risks [threats], and the thorough and detailed documentation of the external and internal situation will help your company stay on solid ground.

Current Marketing Situation: This section compares the current business trends with your internal and external analyses, and this will be measured against your company's SWOT (Internal Strengths and Weaknesses, External Opportunities and Threats). This section will cover the existing products, markets, competitors and any other environmental forces that affect the business both inside and out.

Objectives & Issues: Here you will outline the specific marketing objectives you want your business to achieve and the issues that affect its ability to achieve them.

Target Market: This section explains why you are targeting a specific demographic category of the market and how you plan to reach it.

Marketing Strategy: This part is where you give specific details about the marketing strategies you are currently using and will implement in the future to accomplish your business objectives and achieve your sales goals.

Marketing Programs: This is an outline of the programs supporting your marketing strategies. Each marketing program description should detail the specific activities to be carried out and what needs to be done in the areas of product, price, place, promotion, and service to meet or exceed the goals of the marketing strategy it embodies.

Financial Plans: This section reveals your anticipated revenues, expenses, and profits based on the activities and plans in your marketing programs.

Implementation Controls: The implementation controls must indicate how progress towards your marketing strategies will be measured and how adjustments will be made to keep the programs on track.

PRIMARY MARKETING TOOLS

There is a primary set of tools that you need to consider and utilize to make marketing planning more efficient and effective:

Product Offering: A product is usually a tangible item or a service, but it can be both. Tangible items are like paintings, figurines, shirts, shoes, etc; services include massage, insurance, and coaching. Self-help books, eyeglasses, smoke detectors, musical instruments, toys, and computers are examples of products that are both because they are products yet they offer a corresponding service for their users.

Pricing: Correctly pricing your products and services requires an intimate understanding of all the costs involved with creating and providing them to your customers.

Channel: This is the vehicle or method through which the purchased product is delivered. There are many ways to handle this now depending on what you are selling, e.g. books can be bought digitally, music is now available as downloadable files through various sources, etc.

Promotion: The various ways of introducing your brand, product, or services to the world. Anything that goes into communicating your product's features and/or value to potential customers falls into this category. This includes press releases, blog postings, social media, direct selling, email marketing, online shopping sites, etc.

ON TO THE STEPS

We will now move on to the seven steps you need to undertake to craft an integrated and implementable marketing plan. The description of these steps will detail methods for obtaining the data and documentation mentioned in the previous chapter and will give tips and methods to keep your marketing plan updated.

1- Analyze Your Current Situation

2- Research Markets and Customers

3- Establish Segments, Targets and Positions

4- Detail Objectives and Direction

5- Determine Strategies and Programs

6- Track Progress and Activities

7- Evolve and Control Your Plan

STEP 1 – ANALYZE YOUR CURRENT SITUATION

The first step to creating a marketing plan is to study the current location and surrounding market and industry terrain so you can understand the landscape and, ultimately, chart a course.

External Research: This section must be created in detail and will require in-depth notes, thoughts and brainstorming covering your geographic boundaries, competitors, customers you currently sell to, distribution channels that you have, demographic data, and information pertaining to trends in your current markets that are product-related and demographic-related. It should also include anticipated trends due to documented (and some undocumented) changes in the economic, technological, political-legal, ecological, and social-cultural forces that could potentially affect marketing, performance, and profits.

The employees in customer relations and sales should be able to easily answer the following questions:

1- What are your current products or services?

2- What are your current product lines or service lines?

3- What is the approximate dollar size of your current market or markets?

4- What is your sales set-up?

5- What is your distribution set-up?

6- To what geographic area do you sell?

7- What is the population of your audience?

8- What are the income levels of your audience?

9- What competitors do you have in this marketplace? Who do you regularly compete with or lose business to?

10- How well have your products sold in the past?

As your business grows, the management team should continue to track this information, but for now you must create this detailed document to establish a baseline. The marketing plan is where you can pull all relevant information together and justify your actions for the upcoming year, and in some cases beyond. In the marketing plan, you should consider how each of your services or products compares to the services and products of your major competitors [also include any up-and-coming competitors with unique, yet unrealized, ideas]. You should explore whether there are opportunities within the market that neither you nor your competition is currently exploring (or exploiting).

Internal Research: Finding the strengths, weaknesses, opportunities, and threats (SWOT) of your business isn't easy, and this is where your business plan will come in handy.

While reading through your business plan, make a list of all the strengths and opportunities you can think of. Try to be as critical and specific as possible. Think of what makes your products and services better, different, or more valuable, from reasonable prices to durability as well as key benefits and how you can improve further. Afterwards, make a new list and this time think of your business from an outsider's point of view to document weaknesses and probable threats facing your company, i.e., products being too heavy, services taking too long to finish or similar items sold from competitors that may be more appealing to customers.

The process of building the SWOT Analysis of your business is the first step to creating your comprehensive marketing plan; once you find out what these are, you will naturally want to make full use of the strengths and opportunities and find ways to minimize weaknesses and threats.

In addition to understanding this information, there are always good and bad implications within the current market. You should consider the following questions when determining the opportunities and threats in the current market:

1- Which trends in the market are working against you? How can you overcome them?

2- Are there threatening competitive trends? How can you utilize these trends to improve your situation?

3- Are your current products prepared for success in your target markets as they exist right now?

4- Which marketplace trends are working in your favor? How can we enhance these beneficial effects?

5- Are your current marketplace demographics working for or against you?

This information can be found just about anywhere. You can begin with city and state business publications, and you can talk with local business reporters and browse chambers of commerce publications. You can also contact various manufacturers, read trade journals, or talk to professionals you know.

If your company is simply creating a marketing plan for the coming year, it is important to address issues which were discovered during the previous year in an effort to create and implement strategies to overcome them.

Also, while preparing to write the marketing plan, you will discover that different members of your company will have different ideas about the current situation and the elements therein. You can use this opportunity to compare different aspects of the market against one another.

STEP 2 – RESEARCH MARKETS AND CUSTOMERS

When you were creating your business plan, you developed a general idea of the target markets that may be most interested in the products and services you have to offer. With your marketing plan, you can hone in on your target market and the best way to reach them.

The first step is to focus on the benefits of your products. Each product may cater to a different target market: this one may be more interesting to teenagers and young adults, while another may be more helpful for young mothers or stay-at-home caregivers. Remember that your target market should be the one with the strongest or most compelling need for your product.

Knowing your target market will also help you narrow down the countless marketing strategies available so you know which ones might be more effective. For example, if your product is geared towards customers in their teens and twenties, you can probably use the Internet to reach them, while media such as magazines and televisions commercials may be better to market items targeting more mature women.

Determining your target market will take research, but with the quick access to information provided by the Internet, this task will prove far less tricky than it used to be. You can conduct online surveys to get more details about what your potential customers are truly interested in. Aside from online research, why not put your family and friends on the spot and ask them what they think? The more you know about your target market, the better. Some of the basic information you may require includes:

- **Age** (people of different age groups or generations have different needs and desires)

- **Gender** (men and women often require different products and services or respond to a different approach to marketing these products)

- **Location** (details such as climate, temperature, proximity to mountains or bodies of water, etc)

- **Education** (people with different educational backgrounds require different tools and services)

- **Income level** (those with higher income are more likely to go for luxurious and expensive items that they want; not necessarily need)

- **Marital status** (married couples often have different priorities than singles)

- **Family life cycle** (the needs of families with infants differ from those with teenagers)

- **Occupation/profession** (those in blue collar positions may differ in their wants from those in white collar professions for some items)

- **Ethnicity** (people of various cultures differ in the products and services they want)

- **Religious beliefs** (some religions have restrictions on clothing, beauty products, etc)

- **Social class** (upper-, middle-, and lower-class groups have differing interests)

Researching Your Market: It is important to research your market thoroughly so you have relevant data when solving marketing problems for your company or for specific products and services. If your company is just starting up, then this is an absolute necessity. Thorough surveys of the market function as the cornerstone for any successful business planning.

Without market research, you cannot identify specific segments within your market nor will you see how your products and services differ from those of your competitors. Whether you use experimental methods, survey methods, observational methods, or historical methods, you will end up with two types of data.

The first is primary which is gathered by an outside source but compiled by you. The secondary data is both compiled and organized by someone else. Secondary research is the most popular source of information generally used by government agencies, businesses within the industry, or trade associations. It takes less time to find and, if recently completed by a reliable source, is just as good—if not better—than research you might undertake yourself.

Primary Research: Primary research can be either exploratory or specific.

- Exploratory research is indefinite or unrestricted, allowing you to define a specific problem better. It will require detailed and unstructured interviews which include lengthy answers from respondents.

- Specific research is carried out to solve a problem identified by exploratory research. The interviews are structured and very formal, making it the more expensive of the two.

- If you plan to conduct primary research with your own resources, the first step is deciding how to question your target group. You can do this through direct mail, telemarketing, or personal interviews (as a few examples).

Direct Mail: Email may be far easier, but don't forget about offline marketing, Response rate for direct mail is generally less than three percent, but some signs suggest that it is having a resurgence in popularity. Humans used to toss "junk mail" aside without even looking at it; now we have started to long for an envelope or glossy postcard addressed to us. A combination of the two may also work well, e.g. mailing out a postcard with an introduction to an online survey may get an even higher response rate than either of those items alone.

If you are using direct mail, there are a few means and methods you can use to enhance your rate of response and increase the quality of your responses.

1- Keep it brief

2- Specify a recipient by name on your address label

3- Keep your survey/questionnaire to two pages or less

4- Explain what the survey is for in a brief note to the

recipient

5- Mail out a reminder approximately one and a half weeks after the original mailing and include a self-addressed, postage paid envelope for ease of return

Phone Surveys: Phone surveys are cost-effective and usually offer a higher response rate. The best part about phone surveys is that you can cover a wider geographic area especially since phone rates are extremely manageable. The cost is one third that of personal interviews, whose response rate rests around 10 percent. There are certain requirements to keep in mind it you want to implement a successful market research campaign using phone surveys.

1- The name of the respondent must be confirmed before any discussion takes place

2- The interviewer must minimize pauses in order to maintain energy and flow of the survey

3- A follow-up call should be scheduled if information needs to be confirmed or added

4- Any information referring to the topic of the survey or the reason for the research should not be divulged until the survey is completed satisfactorily

Personal Interviews: There are two kinds of personal interviews. There are group workshops and in-depth interviews.

The **group workshop** is often the course of action for a larger organization and is used for brainstorming product strengths and weaknesses and suggesting product modifications.

The **in-depth interview** is conducted in a one-on-one setting where the interview works off of a short checklist. These interview methods can range from non-directive to topic focused.

Costs: When you consider which method should be used, bear in mind the costs that come with them.

There are some obvious costs for mailings, such as envelopes, postage, paper and printing. In addition there is time spent for collateral development, research analysis and validation of results. Telephone surveys remove the cost for printed collateral and mailing pieces, but costs need to still consider survey development and staff time (i.e., interviewer, analyst, project management). Personal interviews and group workshops will incur a mix of these costs.

This is a great start but your needs may vary, depending on the products you have and the target market you are aiming at. After getting all the information you need, you can then create a customer demographic profile so you can easily pinpoint which product suits which target market best.

Getting the interest of your target market is one thing; keeping the attention permanently is another. This is why you also need psychographic information comprising hobbies, activities, interests, attitudes and personalities of your target market. Your customer demographic profile will narrow down your target market, and the psychographic information you have gathered will then help you fine-tune your marketing strategies directly towards it.

STEP 3 – ESTABLISH SEGMENTS, TARGETS AND POSITIONS

I believe it was Abraham Lincoln who said it best: "You can please some of the people some of the time; all of the people some of the time; some of the people all of the time; but you can never please all of the people all of the time."

Well, not to ride on Honest Abe's coat tails, but he was right. No organization can be all things to all people, which is why marketers must apply their knowledge of the market and their existing customers to determine which parts of the market should be targeted for marketing campaigns and strategic initiatives.

The purpose of segmentation is to group customers with similar needs, wants, behavior, or other characteristics that affect their demand for or usage of the goods or services you are marketing.

Once your customers have been segmented, you can then focus on the following questions:

1-   Are you marketing to one segment, several segments, or the entire market?

2-   If several, which ones?

3-   How will you cover each of these segments?

The next step is then to formulate a suitable position for your product within each segment. This means making your product unique to easily differentiate it from competing products in the same market. This is known as the unique selling proposition or differentiator, and it must be based on a benefit that the consumer will receive; otherwise it will be meaningless and forgettable. If you can solve a problem or ease some "pain" your potential customers are feeling—and you can get that message across quickly and clearly through your marketing efforts—your consumers are more likely to come straight to you and keep coming back.

STEP 4 – DETAIL OBJECTIVES AND DIRECTION

At this point, you have now become more than what you have been—you are responsible for setting the direction of your company's marketing activities by setting goals and objectives.

Goals: Longer-term performance targets for the organization.

Objectives: Shorter-term performance targets that support the achievement of the organization's goals.

You may decide to concentrate on brand awareness and use strategies geared towards earning higher sales volume and increasing web traffic to your company website, or you may focus on relationship marketing to get new customers and make sure they keep coming back for your products and services.

Your marketing plan should cover the specifics of each marketing strategy that you plan to carry out, and that way you will know better whether your goals are realistic or not. Remember to set goals that are S.M.A.R.T.—specific, measurable, attainable, relevant, and time-bound. This makes it easier for you to have a clear idea of your marketing strategies and know exactly what to do to carry them out well.For example: If you are in marketing, it doesn't help if you keep talking about how good your marketing company is. It doesn't matter how efficient your marketing division is or how impressive your company's background may be.

Chances are if you are with a good company, your prospect knows your company's reputation. The key questions on your prospect's mind are:

- *Why should we bring our business to you over your competitor down the street?*

- *What can you do for me that your competitors can't?*

- *What can YOU offer that will set you apart from the others?*

It's very important that you remember that people buy from YOU, not just the company and not just a product! So when you're trying to stand out in a crowded marketplace, don't just focus on the features, advantages, and benefits of your product or service and expect them to be sold on it. Focus on what your product can do for your customer, and most importantly concentrate your efforts on what YOU personally can do for them.

STEP 5 – DETERMINE STRATEGIES AND PROGRAMS

To know what to do, you need to plan, and a marketing plan will help you map out what you need to do to ensure your company's success. A marketing plan should cover an entire year. Don't think of it as a list of things to accomplish before the year is over, but rather as a guide that will also help you prioritize what is important. For example, you may have different products and a whole bunch of strategies for each, but working on a limited budget means that you cannot execute them all at once. You need to determine which products should be marketed first and the strategies that will work best for each.

The input from the different departments/branches of your company can be very valuable in deciding which products and strategies to prioritize. It's not just the sales and marketing team of your company who can help create a good marketing plan. The accounting, manufacturing, secretarial, and other branches should also be involved too. The different experiences, educational achievements and social backgrounds of the people in those areas can provide valuable information and advice that may not occur to you or the marketing team.

Marketing strategies and programs must be consistent with your organization's overall direction, goals, and strategies. External marketing strategies should also be established for the supply chain and distribution channel to build relationships with suppliers, partners, and channel partners. Your company needs an internal marketing strategy, proper staffing for carrying out marketing programs, and customer care that is consistent with the established strategy and positioning.

For each marketing strategy you use, consider the five Cs—consumer, channel, company, competition, and climate. Although your products will have a specific target market in mind, you can aim to gain the interest of potential consumers in different ways, hence the unique channel or strategy you need to get to them. However, bear in mind that your goal should always be to promote your company, for you want your clients to be interested not just in one product but everything else you have to offer. In order to rise above your competition, you need to study the economic, social, and cultural climate of the target market you are aiming for. If you consider the five Cs of each marketing strategy, you will be able to keep track of which ones are working out and which ones need to be modified.

To help you prioritize what is important, remember to make sure that the vision statement of your company is included in your marketing plan. Your vision statement should detail the pending objectives for your business, and adding it to your marketing plan will help you stay on track and keep you inspired throughout the implementation phase.

STEP 6 – TRACK PROGRESS AND ACTIVITIES

Once strategies and programs are implemented, tracking mechanisms must be developed and put in place—metrics must be established to measure progress—in order to determine effectiveness. Most companies will use sales forecasts, budgets, schedules, and other tools to record standards against which progress can be measured.

By comparing actual results against daily, weekly, monthly, quarterly, and yearly projections, management can see the areas where the company is experiencing success, where it is stagnant or losing ground, and where it needs to make adjustments to get back on track.

Every day you spend working on your business will lead to modifications, successes, and failures in your marketing strategies, and it is important to record all of these events. Keep track of the results of your sales, budgets, presentations, phone calls, website posts, website page views, articles, engagements, discounts and offers, etc. Even if you don't have the time each day to edit or update your marketing plan and add the recent occurrences and new results of your strategies, you should note them down so you can revise your plan easily the next time.

It is also important to observe what competitors are doing through the course of this review process and where the market is heading so you can put your results into context and have a frame of reference from which to improve your efforts.

STEP 7 – EVOLVE AND CONTROL YOUR PLAN

The greatest marketing plan in the world is useless without effective implementation, as numerous businesses—both online and offline—have learned in a not so nice way.

To keep your marketing plan "well" implemented, you should start with the objectives that have been established and the corresponding measurement processes, and track the performance of the marketing programs. Note the results, and then take corrective action if results fail to measure up to the anticipated criteria. This is the marketing control process.

The marketing control process is iterative or repetitive; managers will need to repeatedly retrace their steps as they assess the results of the marketing strategies. Companies use this control process to analyze their marketing implementation on the basis of such measures as market share, sales, profitability, and productivity.

As your business grows, changes, and improves, so should your marketing plan. A marketing strategy that worked well for you in the early days may not be suitable when your business is in a growth phase or has plateaued on a certain level of success. For example, calling up clients one by one is fine when your company is still in launch mode, but email and having your own company newsletter is much better once you have more than a hundred customers. You need to adapt to the changing business landscape, and you also need to edit your plan. Remove unsuccessful strategies to accommodate others that are more suited to the consumer needs at the time.

Marketing plans should be referred to monthly and updated quarterly (at the very least), especially in the early phases of your business where advertising strategies and new changes become rapidly evident. Don't think of your marketing plan as something you need to accomplish or complete on a deadline. As your company grows, your marketing plan needs to be updated and revised along with it, so stay flexible and think of your regular marketing plan updates as a welcome task to improve your company and find new ways to market your products better.

No marketing plan is perfect from the time it is drafted, but as you continue to make necessary revisions, it can become more and more in tune with the present situation of your company's marketing efforts. In time, it will become an easily implementable marketing plan that will effectively present important facts such as the growth potential of all your products and services, quarterly profits and losses, and the costs for the marketing strategies detailed in the marketing plan. Take time each month to ensure your marketing plan is up-to-date, implementable and integrated, and you will find it an invaluable resource as your business improves and expands.

BONUSES & EXTRAS

The 5 Guiding Principles of Marketing

Now that you know the seven essential steps to writing an integrated and implementable marketing plan, we will discuss how you can maintain your marketing strengths through the implementation of five broad principles. These are not just tasks to be accomplished or items on a to-do list; these are mantras or ideals that should be incorporated into every aspect of your business life—and if you are an entrepreneur…all aspects of your personal life as well. But applying these directly to your business will contribute to the value of your products and services and help your organization remain competitive.

Maintain Vigilance: To say that the economy has gone global is an understatement. Business is transacted faster than ever, and the barriers to entry in most markets have been reduced—or even eliminated. Online businesses are prevalent, and your competition is going to be fierce. The only way to truly get through these challenges is to remain vigilant in your efforts and don't give up.

Remain Focused on Relationships: The wide range of choices available for customers make it easier for them to find exactly what they want for the price that they are willing to pay. When your service or product is in direct competition with another's, the deal breaker could be the strength of your relationship with that customer. By offering value to your customers and clients and opening a door for continuous two-way communication, you will create a large group of repeat customers. People don't care how much you know until they know how much you care, so make sure they know that you care about their needs and want to solve their problems.

Keep Everyone Involved: Sales and marketing are no longer the sole responsibility of the business developers and marketers. Everyone in the company is a representative of the firm. Every contact that is made with a customer is a chance to instill further value to the client. Being satisfied with you (client satisfaction) will keep them from taking a serious look at your competitors—although they will most likely take a look…human nature and all.

Seek and Establish Alliances: No man is an island, right? No company is one either. If you want to make things a little easier, establish alliances with people in your industry who either control the work or know where new opportunities can be found. If you can come to the table with some way to assist them in return, then the relationship becomes much easier and success for all involved parties is inevitable.

Be Innovative and Creative: The old way of doing things is no longer (or not always) the best way. In most cases, there are newer, more effective, more efficient ways of accomplishing various tasks—all with the objective of helping you to work smarter and faster. This type of creativity and innovation in your products and services will also bring more customers and clients to your doorstep. Don't get stuck in a traditional thought process; if you have an idea, don't let it go until you have tried it—chances are it will probably work.

Size Matters

The first question that will come up from the designated author of a marketing plan—who is most likely terrified at the thought of writing such an "intimidating" document—is "how long does the plan need to be?" The page count of your marketing plan will fluctuate as you add information and update sections. But the base size should be a direct reflection of the size of your company. A smaller company should have a brief, yet comprehensive plan. A multi-national organization will have marketing plans for each distinct department, division, or product. There is no hard and fast rule here; just make sure you are not taking shortcuts as this document should be the guide for the upcoming year. Don't forget, your plan needs regular reviews and updates. [Weekly is best, but unlikely for various, and obvious, reasons.]

The ideal marketing plan should be a blueprint for the upcoming year. It is limited to one year as today's marketplaces change rapidly and you may find that new promotions don't work after a very short time and you will need to make adjustments and updates on a more frequent basis; But although regular updates are essential, review and realignment of your marketing plan must occur when your organization's business plan is updated—once a year. A section can be placed in the marketing plan for monthly reports on things such as sales and manufacturing for performance tracking. It is also recommended that your plan touch on events/promotions/product plans, etc for in longer-term segments—perhaps covering a two- or four-year span. This is not entirely necessary as it is more important for your plan to focus on the 12-month span. The time frame covered by your plan should be the full calendar year or your firms' fiscal year, if they do not coincide.

Development: It may take around two months to write a marketing plan at this level, and that's even before finalizing and publishing it. But this is a guesstimate as the most difficult part of this process is developing the plan and detailing it on paper. Execution of your approved marketing plan will create some challenges, but your largest issue is determining how your organization will bring products/services to market.

Involvement: It is important for all employees to have access to your approved marketing plan. There is no reason for an organization to keep a marketing plan secret; there are very few—if any—secrets to protect from competitors anymore. The age of the information superhighway has changed that. But marketing efforts are never successful without the involvement or buy-in of all staff members. Whatever size your organization is, employee feedback should not just be accepted, but encouraged and seriously considered in the context of updating the marketing plan to meet the needs of the market and your staff.

By allowing all employees to contribute in one way or another, they all feel as though they are a part of the organization's goals and integral to its success, and as such, are willing to work harder to see projects that they have contributed to achieve success. Employees are more motivated to perform for the organization in which they feel valued, since they know that their ideas are an overall part of improving the organization. Taking advantage of decision-making from all employees will create the opportunity for advanced creativity and also ensures better division of labor.

Managers can be encouraged to use their own teams, and each team can then be responsible for different parts when reviewing the marketing plan. You can also have a cross-functional team that works within all divisions, ensuring that all employees are performing tasks and continually challenging them in their jobs and in working well with one another.

By facilitating better communication, your company will be able to improve efficiency within departments. Your divisions must continually be in sync with one another, and this in turn contributes to more efficiency and effectiveness in workplace processes and staff functions.

Your top levels will still maintain the overall say in major company decisions, but the smaller divisions are included in the individual aspects, all of which combine to make a large and impressive organization work from the bottom upward instead of from the top downward. This is the best way to ensure great marketing and company involvement.

Competition: Your competition should also be evaluated and details included, i.e., who they are, what products/services do they sell, which feature or benefits of those products/services are they utilizing as the main point of their marketing campaigns, how are they pricing these products/services, how are they packaging them, and in today's markets, how are they being delivered. This is also the best place to discuss how your firm differs from the competitors and detail it in the form of a SWOT analysis for ease of review and comparison.

In your target market and segmentation section, you should be able to create a profile of your perfect customer which includes demographic information, hobbies, favorite colors, books, job type, residential information, etc. There are always one-offs in your customer base, but you can add to the customer profiles as you go. It is also best to include information as you discover it for each target marketing or consumer segment including price point, packaging preferences, preferred delivery methods, etc.

Evaluation: When you are evaluating your marketing plan, consider your criteria and measures of success, the completion of action timeframes and deadlines, accomplishment of goals and strategies and results. Also take into account new customers, repeat customers, average size of contracts/engagements, and revenue.

CONCLUSION

Your marketing plan should address the short-term (1 to 12 months) as well as touch on the long-term (over 12 months), so it should outline the major goals of the year while also analyzing the mechanics necessary to meet those goals, and this brings together the short-term actions to meet the established objectives along with the long-term goals. It is good to think beyond the upcoming year and include the next few years in your comprehensive planning process.

With an integrated and implementable marketing plan, you should be able to anticipate

- how many employees you will add over the upcoming years

- how much office space you may need

- whether your staff needs additional training or unique certifications

- whether or not you will be purchasing major equipment

- how to improve your profit margins

- how to become active in local, regional, and national trade groups

- how the market demographics will affect your business in the future

Overall, an integrated, implementable marketing plan acts as the key ingredient in the recipe for a successful business. We hope that this guide will help you create the best marketing plan for your business and that it continues to prove itself a valuable asset in the years to come.

ABOUT THE AUTHOR

Cassandra Fenyk is a dynamic marketer, speaker, and motivator with extensive experience in various B2B and B2C industries, and unlike many other website and social media consultants, she is also an established marketing professional with nearly 20 years of experience in developing and directing business-to-consumer and business-to-business market penetration strategies. She has spent the majority of her career entrenched in branding, messaging, strategic planning, and project management. She has a keen understanding of the selling process and the critical steps between the initial message, the final sale, and post-sale relationship maintenance. Combined with her knowledge and experience in managing social media and website SEO programs, these traits make her a great source of information and an invaluable resource for your business.

Most recently, Ms. Fenyk started her coaching business focusing on start-ups, small businesses, and entrepreneurs; and all the characteristics that entails. Shark Bite Coaching (www.sharkbitecoaching.com) is that business and if you would like more personalized assistance in avoiding common business pitfalls, overcoming obstacles to your business growth, and getting your business moving in the right direction, ask her and set up an appointment to discuss your ideas and goals.

RECOMMENDED READING LIST

15 Marketing Trends In 2013 And How Your Business Can Use Them
Rohit Bhargava

Sexy Little Numbers: How to Grow Your Business Using the Data You Already Have
Dimitri Maex & Paul B. Brown

Marketing to Millennials: Reach the Largest and Most Influential Generation of Consumers Ever
Jeff Fromm & Christie Garton

The Branded Mind: What Neuroscience Really Tells Us About the Puzzle of the Brain and the Brand
Erik Du Plessis

Breakthrough Marketing Plans: How to Stop Wasting Time and Start Driving Growth
Tim Calkins

The Tipping Point: How Little Things Can Make a Big Difference
Malcolm Gladwell

LOOK FOR MORE BUSINESS-BUILDING AND BUSINESS EXCELLENCE BOOKS BY SHARK BITE COACHING ON AMAZON

Shark Bite Coaching
PO Box 373
Florham Park, NJ 07932
shark@sharkbitecoaching.com

A Note to the Reader:

This manual is intended to give guidance on the seven most important steps to take in the creation and implementation of a comprehensive marketing plan for your business. Consult your attorney, tax accountant, or other professional advisors before choosing the right path for you and your business.